BY APPOINTMENT TO H.M. THE QUEEN
MANUFACTURERS OF CHUTNEY & PURVEYORS OF INDIAN
CURRY POWDER. J. A. SHARWOOD & CO. LTD. LONDON.

Sharwood's

Sharwood's offers you these menus as appropriate to most circumstances, from an instant 'Indian Supper' with family or friends to a formal 'Indian Celebration' for larger gatherings.

The cooking techniques may seem simple, and the ingredients familiar, but the mouthwatering aromas and delicious flavours of each dish come from the forty or so powders, pickles, chutneys, sauces, pastes, accompaniments and condiments of all descriptions, now so readily available. Each distills a century's experience and will transform your ability to enjoy such delights in your own home.

The charm of Indian food lies in the spicing, which must enhance yet never overpower. Sharwood's offers its observations on these precious seeds, fruits, leaves and berries on the penultimate page.

James Allen Sharwood; founder, traveller, linguist and gourmet was above all an adventurer. It is hoped, in some small way, to recreate his spirit as we go forward into the realm of Indian food.

TRADITIONAL

 ## Cucumber Raita

Cut the cucumber into dice, sprinkle with salt and allow to drain for 15 minutes. Mix into the yoghurt in a dish. Serve chilled.

½ cucumber
1 teaspoon salt
1 carton natural yoghurt (5fl oz)

Palak Aloo

Sauté the onions. Stir in salt and Garam Masala. Add the potatoes and spinach, cover and cook for approximately 15 minutes or until potato is tender.

2 onions, finely chopped
50g butter (2oz)
1 teaspoon salt, 2 heaped teaspoons Sharwood's Garam Masala Curry Spices
750g potatoes peeled, par-boiled and cut in quarters (1½lb)
250g frozen spinach thawed (8oz)

Serves 6 as an accompaniment.

Chicken Kashmir

Blend the Kashmir Sauce Mix, yoghurt and lime juice. Add the chicken and coat evenly. Refrigerate for 2 hours. Sauté the onion, add the chicken and marinade. Cover and simmer gently for approximately 1 hour until tender. Place the chicken on a serving dish. Blend the cooking liquid with the soured cream and heat through. Pour the sauce over the chicken. Serve with Basmati Rice and garnish with lime slices.

6 chicken drumsticks, skinned
1 sachet Sharwood's Kashmir Mild Curry Sauce Mix
2 tablespoons natural yoghurt
Juice of 1 lime or lemon
1 onion, peeled and sliced in rings
25g butter (1oz)
4 tablespoons soured cream
½ packet Sharwood's Basmati Rice
1 lime, sliced

Serves 6 as a main dish.

Parathas

Shape and cook according to the packet instructions.

1 packet Sharwood's Chapati, Paratha and Puri Mix
Oil
Water

Beef and Coconut Curry

Quickly stir-fry beef in extremely hot oil un brown. Add onions and garlic and fry gently for 5 minutes. Add the Curry Powder and co gently for 2 minutes. Blend the coconut with the hot water and stir into the curry. Add Chutney and salt. Either simmer gently for approximately 2 hours, or add a little more water and pressure cook at 'H' for 15 minute

750g chuck steak or shin beef, cubed (1½lb)
2 tablespoons, oil
2 onions, peeled, sliced
2 cloves garlic, chopped
4 heaped teaspoons Sharwood's Hot or Extr Hot Curry Powder
50g Sharwood's Creamed Coconut (2oz)
1 tablespoon Sharwood's Major Grey Chut Pinch of salt
125ml hot water (¼ pint)

Serves 6 with accompaniments.

COUNTRY

Colonel Skinner's Fancy

Line a 21cm (8 inch) pie dish with part of the pastry. Mix the mutton, chutney, cornflour, parsley and seasoning and spoon into the pastry case. Roll remaining pastry to cover the pie. Seal well and use trimmings to decorate. Glaze with the beaten egg. Bake for 1-1½ hours (180°C, 350°F, Gas Mark 4). Serve hot or cold.

350g shortcrust pastry (12oz)
500g mutton cubed (1lb)
4 tablespoons Sharwood's Mango Chutney
1 tablespoon cornflour
1 tablespoon parsley, chopped
2 teaspoons salt
Freshly ground black pepper
Egg to glaze

Serves 6 as a main dish.

Coconut Pudding

Bring the milk and sugar to the boil. Set aside. Blend the creamed coconut with the melted butter in a pan and heat for 5 minutes. Now add the milk and leave to thicken over a low heat stirring all the time. When the milk has been reduced by half add the dry fruits and rose water. Leave to cool before serving. Garnish with almonds.

75g caster sugar (3oz)
850ml creamy milk (1½ pints)
50g unsalted butter (2oz)
100g Sharwood's Creamed Coconut (4oz)
25g sultanas (2oz)
2 tablespoons rose water
25g flaked almonds (2oz), toasted

Serves 6.

Pork and Apricot Tiffin

Cut the pork into small rounds ¾″ thick, coat with seasoned flour and brown in the oil. Add ½ jar of Hot Curry Paste, ¼ pint of water, apricot syrup and lime juice. Cover and braise for 1 hour (180°C, 350°F, Gas Mark 4). Stir in Apricots and more water if needed, return to the oven for 10 minutes. Serve garnished with coriander leaves.

2 small tenderloins of pork, or 750g lean pork (1½lb)
2 tablespoons wholemeal flour
1 teaspoon salt
1 teaspoon oil
½ jar Sharwood's Hot Curry Paste
Juice of 1 lime
¼ pint (140ml) water
1 can Sharwood's Whole Apricots, pitted and drained
Coriander for garnish

Serves 6 as a main dish

Carrot Braise

Sauté the onions in the butter, stir in the Curry Paste and cook for 3 minutes. Add the carrots and coat in the sauce, stir in the water and simmer for 20 minutes.

2 onions peeled and sliced
1oz butter
2 heaped teaspoons Sharwood's Mild or Hot Curry Paste
500g carrots, sliced into 4 (1lb)
3 tablespoons water

Serves 6 as an accompaniment

BARBECUE

Tandoori Chicken

Remove chicken skin and slash flesh several times with a sharp knife. Sprinkle with salt and half the lemon juice. Set aside. Whisk together the Tandoori Mix with the vinegar, oil, remaining lemon juice and yoghurt. Coat chicken with this marinade, cover and leave overnight in a cool place. Grill for 15-20 minutes each side. Serve with lettuce and lemon wedges.

6 chicken portions, skinned
1 sachet Sharwood's Tandoori Barbecue Mix or
4 heaped teaspoons from the orange drum.
Juice of 1 lemon
1 teaspoon salt
3 tablespoons natural yoghurt
3 tablespoons oil
3 tablespoons vinegar
Lemon wedges
Lettuce

Serves 6 with accompaniments.

Shish Kebabs

Knead all ingredients to make a smooth mixture. Divide into 6. Shape 3 to a skewer. Place on a tray and refrigerate for 2 hours. Barbecue or grill for 15-20 minutes. Good hot or cold.

350g minced lamb or beef (12oz)
1 onion, chopped
2 teaspoons lemon juice
2 heaped teaspoons Sharwood's Medium or Hot Curry Powder
1 tablespoon natural yoghurt
1 egg, beaten
2 tablespoons gram or plain flour
2 tablespoons chopped coriander
1½ teaspoons salt

Serves 6 as an accompaniment.

Pasanda Tikka

Thoroughly prick pork and marinate 6 hours in yoghurt, salt and curry paste. Drain, then barbecue 20 minutes and serve brushed with melted butter. Garnish with onion, lemon and serve with Sharwood's Lime Pickle.

350g lean pork, cubed (120oz)
75g Natural yoghurt (½ x 5oz carton)
2 teaspoons salt
4 heaped teaspoons Sharwood's Mild or Hot Curry Paste
75g melted butter (3oz)
2 onions cut into rings
1 lemon, sliced
Sharwood's Lime Pickle

Serves 6 as an accompaniment

Prawns Poona

Slit prawn backs, devein, hinge open and place shell-side uppermost on the barbecue. Cook for 3 minutes until pink. Turn over and place a little of the chutney in each prawn. Continue cooking for 5 minutes. Serve hot.

18 large Pacific prawns, uncooked (frozen or fresh)
6 tablespoons Sharwood's Bengal Hot Chutney

Serves 6 as an accompaniment.

Naan Bread

Shape and cook according to the instructions.

1 packet Sharwood's Naan Bread Mix
Water

N.B. These recipes work as well under the kitchen grill.

SUPPER

Masala Chicken Risotto

Rinse rice thoroughly until water runs clear. Sauté onion until soft, add rice and fry till transparent. Add Garam Masala, tomatoes, salt and ¾ pint stock. Simmer for 10 minutes. Arrange chicken, okra and peppers on top. Cook slowly for 15 minutes so that chicken is steamed through.

½ packet Sharwood's Basmati Rice
2 onions, peeled and diced
50g butter (2oz)
2 heaped teaspoons Sharwood's Garam Masala
½ red pepper, diced
1 can Okra, drained
4 tomatoes, peeled and diced
1 teaspoon salt
250g chicken, cooked and sliced (8oz)
Coriander leaves for garnish

Serves 4 as supper dish.

Kheema Avarai

Place the mince, onions, mushrooms and paste in a pan. Season well. Simmer gently for 1-1½ hours. Add the beans 20 minutes before the end of the cooking time. Serve with jacket potatoes.

500g minced beef (1lb)
1 onion, finely diced
100g button mushrooms, sliced (4oz)
2 teaspoons Sharwood's Mild or Hot Curry Paste
1 teaspoon salt
150g green beans, sliced (6oz)

Serves 4 as supper dish

Bengal Pork Hot Pot

Sauté onions for 2-3 minutes. Stir in the Bengal Sauce Mix, water and chutney, to make a sauce. Add the meat. Lay a covering of potatoes in the base of a buttered casserole dish, add meat and top with a layer of potatoes. Dot with butter and bake for ¾-1 hour (180°C, 350°F, Gas Mark 4.)

2 onions, peeled and sliced
50g butter (2oz)
1 sachet Sharwood's Bengal Hot Curry Sauce Mix
250ml water (½ pint)
3 tablespoons Sharwood's Green Label Mango Chutney
500g lean cooked pork sliced (1 lb)
750g potatoes, peeled, par-boiled (1½lb)

Serves 4 as a supper dish.

Lamb Stuffed Chilli Marrow

Scoop the seeds out of the centre of the marrow rings and place on a greased baking dish. Sauté the onion in the butter, stir in the spices and flour. Add the meat and cook quickly. Stir in the stock and pimiento and season well. Spoon into the marrow rings. Dot each one with butter. Cover with foil. Bake for 1 hour (180°C, 350°F, Gas Mark 4.)

1 large marrow cut into 6 rings
25g butter (1oz)
1 onion, chopped
2 cloves garlic, crushed
3 teaspoons Sharwood's Medium or Hot Curry Powder
1 tablespoon flour
350g cooked lamb, finely chopped (12oz)
125ml stock (¼ pint)
1 small can Sharwood's Pimientos, chopped
50g butter (2oz)

Serves 4 as a supper dish.

LIGHT OF INDIA

Maharaja's Prawn Pilau

Thoroughly rinse half the sachet of rice. Drain. Sauté onion. Add rice and fry gently for 3 minutes. Add stock, half the sachet of spices from Pilau Rice and salt. Simmer 20-25 minutes. Stir in prawns, steam 5 minutes. Garnish with coriander.

½ packet Sharwood's Indian Pilau Rice
1 onion, chopped
3 tablespoons butter
450ml stock (¾ pint)
1 teaspoon salt
250g frozen prawns, thawed (8oz)
3 tablespoons fresh coriander

Serves 6 as an accompaniment.

Chicken Korma

Place chicken in casserole, pour over sauce, cover and bake for 1 hour (180°C, 350°F, Gas Mark 4). Tomatoes may be added 15 minutes before the end of the cooking time.

1lb chicken breast, skinned
1 can Sharwood's Moghulai Korma
4 tomatoes, peeled and sliced (optional)

Serves 3 to 4

Nargissi Kofta

Mix the beef, curry powder, salt and half the parsley. Stir in 2 tablespoons of yoghurt. Leave aside. Divide the mixture into 3 and mould around the eggs, to completely cover. Fry in the oil to brown. Stir in the Vegetable Curry, cover and simmer for ½ hour. Serve with each egg cut in half. Stir the remaining yoghurt into the vegetable mixture and serve with the Nargissi Kofta. Sprinkle with parsley.

750g minced beef (1½lb)
2 <u>heaped</u> teaspoons Sharwood's Medium or Hot Curry Powder
2 teaspoons salt
2 tablespoons parsley, chopped
75ml natural yoghurt (½ × 5oz carton)
3 hard boiled eggs
2 tablespoons oil
1 can Sharwood's Vegetable Curry

Serves 6 with an accompaniment.

Kutherakoi

Quickly stir-fry steak in extremely hot oil until brown. Add onion and gently fry until golden brown. Stir in the Vindaloo sauce and keep warm. Shallow fry the aubergines in batches, in the oil. Layer the meat, sauce and aubergines in a casserole, finishing with a layer of aubergines. Bake for 2 hours (170°C, 325°F, Gas Mark 3).

500g Braising steak – sliced thinly across the grain (1lb)
1 tablespoon oil
4 small onions, sliced
1 can Sharwood's Goan Vindaloo
2 aubergines sliced
Oil for shallow frying

Serves 6 with an accompaniment

Lime and Mango Pickles

Serve in small dishes as traditional accompaniments.

1 jar Sharwood's Lime Pickle
1 jar Sharwood's Mango Pickle

CELEBRATION BUFFET

Loganberry Sharbat

Drain Loganberries. Mix syrup with Grand Marnier and lemon juice, freeze. When ready crush ice and divide into 12 glasses and top with Loganberries.

2 cans Sharwood's Loganberries with their syrup
10 tablespoons Grand Marnier
Juice of ½ lemon

Serves 12.

Bombay Bombe

Line a 20cm (8 inch) greased cake tin with 6 beaten escallops. Season with black pepper. Fill with the stuffing and top with the remaining escallops. Bake for ¾ hour (180°C, 350°F, Gas Mark 4) and cool. Turn out of tin. Dissolve gelatine in water and blend into the mayonnaise, pour partly over Bombe and chill. Serve garnished with black olives and bay leaves.

15g butter (½oz)
8 veal escallops, beaten
Black pepper
Stuffing:
   100g breadcrumbs (4oz)
   100g stoned raisins (4oz)
   75g unsalted butter, melted (3oz)
   1 egg yolk
   100g Mozzarella cheese sliced (4oz)
   50g flaked almonds (2oz)
   1 heaped teaspoon Sharwood's Garam Masala
   2 teaspoons salt
1 sachet gelatine
2 tablespoons hot water
250ml mayonnaise (½ pint)
Black olives, bay leaves

Serves 12 as part of spread.

Fillet Masala

Trim the beef and coat with the spices. Wrap in foil and roast 20-25 minutes (210°C, 425°F, Gas Mark 7). Unwrap and cool. Sauté parsnips gently in oil until tender, add vinegar and Tandoori Spice Mix. Cool. Slice and rearrange as shown. Chill until ready.

1-1¼kg whole fillet of beef (2-2½lb)
1 heaped teaspoon Sharwood's Garam Masala
2 teaspoons ground black pepper
500g parsnips, peeled, sliced in sticks (1lb)
3 tablespoons Olive Oil
1½ tablespoons Sharwood's Tarragon Vinegar
1 teaspoon Sharwood's Tandoori Spice Mix

Serves 12 as part of a spread.

Crème Kerala

Drain the salmon, removing any bones. Whip cream, when stiff fold in lemon juice and rind, Curry Powder, Tandoori Spice Mix and salmon. Divide into 12 glasses and chill. Quarter the Puppodums, damping if necessary. Fry 2-3 seconds in extremely hot oil. Cool and drain. Serve Puppodums to dip into salmon. (Puppodums may be stored in an airtight container, for several days).

1 × 439g can red salmon (15oz)
250ml double cream (½ pint)
Rind and juice of a lemon
1 heaped teaspoon Sharwood's Mild or Medium Madras Curry Powder
1 teaspoon Sharwood's Tandoori Spice Mix
12 Sharwood's Plain Puppodums
Oil for deep frying

Serves 12 as a buffet starter.

FEAST

Puppodums

Dip a pair of puppodums back to back in extremely hot oil for 2-3 seconds, and turn them over, drain and keep warm.

2 packets Sharwood's Puppodums
Oil for deep frying

Pig Stick Ribs

Sauté the ribs in the butter. Stir in the sauce and simmer for 1 hour until the sauce has reduced and the flesh is tender.

1 kg Chinese spare ribs of pork (2lb)
50g butter (2oz)
1 can Sharwood's Goan Vindaloo

Serves 12 as part of feast

Almond Kulfi

Whisk all the ingredients together in a liquidizer. Pour into a plastic freezer container and freeze overnight.

2 large tins evaporated milk
100g blanched almonds (4oz)
12 tablespoons caster sugar
2 tablespoons brandy or ½ teaspoon vanilla essence

Serves 12.

Maharanee's Biryani

Marinate lamb preferably overnight. Sauté onions, drain and place in casserole. Drain and fry lamb for 4 minutes stirring frequently and add to onions. Rinse whole sachet of rice. Drain, mix with salt and sachet of spices. Pile on top of lamb. Add boiling stock, cover tightly and bake (180°C, 350°F, Gas Mark 4) for 1 hour. Garnish with raisins and almonds.

1kg lean lamb, diced (2lb)
Marinade:
*   300g natural yoghurt (10oz)*
*   6 heaped teaspoons Sharwood's Mild or*
*   Medium Curry Powder*
*   2 teaspoons salt*
*   2 tablespoons lime juice*
2 onions sliced
100g butter (4oz)
1 packet Sharwood's Pilau Rice
1 teaspoon salt
500ml stock (1 pint)
50g raisins (2oz)
50g flaked almonds (2oz)

Serves 12 as part of feast.

Jingha Malaicurry

Fry onions, add the Creamed Coconut and Curry Sauce Mix. Fry gently for 2-3 minutes. Add the salt, sugar, yoghurt and water. Simmer, covered for 20-25 minutes. Add fish and continue cooking for 10 minutes. Garnish with the onions.

4 tablespoons butter
2 onions, sliced
50g Sharwood's Creamed Coconut (2oz)
1 sachet Sharwood's Bengal Hot Curry Sauce Mix
1 teaspoon salt
½ teaspoon sugar
4 tablespoons natural yoghurt
250ml water (½ pint)
1kg (2lb) peeled prawns or white fish or 2 quarts of mussels steamed and shelled
Fried onions for garnish

Serves 12 as part of feast.

Chick Cheeri Chiri

Cut the chicken into pieces and marinate for 4-5 hours. Drain. Grill for 20 minutes till lightly brown.

Serves 12 as part of feast

1kg lean chicken meat, boned and skinned (2lb)
Marinade:
4 heaped teaspoons Sharwood's Mild or Hot Curry Paste
6 tablespoons oil
1 onion, finely chopped
2 cloves garlic, crushed
Pinch salt
2 tablespoons Sharwood's Tomato Purée

PICNIC

Coral Cushion

Sauté onions in butter, add mushrooms, potatoes and peas. Cook for 5 minutes. Beat eggs, milk, spice and herbs together. Add the vegetables. Bake in a buttered dish for 30 minutes (190°C, 375°F, Gas Mark 5). Cool. Cut in wedges.

2 onions, diced
50g butter (2oz)
75g button mushrooms, sliced (3oz)
2 potatoes, diced
100g peas (4oz)
4 eggs, beaten
4-5 tablespoons creamy milk
1 teaspoon Sharwood's Tandoori Spice Mix
1 tablespoon mixed herbs

Serves 8 with accompaniment.

Coronation Turkey

Remove the skin from the turkey. Combine the dressing ingredients and coat the turkey. Place in a suitable container and sprinkle with the pistachios. Serve with lettuce.

500g cooked turkey, cubed (1lb)
Dressing:
    6 tablespoons Sharwood's Mayonnaise
    3 tablespoons Sharwood's Mild or Medium Curry Powder
    2 tablespoons coriander, chopped
    Juice 1 lemon
100g shelled pistachio nuts (4oz)

Serves 8 with accompaniments.

Medal Mushrooms

Cut the stalks from the mushrooms and wipe the tops. Mix the dressing ingredients together, add the chopped stalks. Combine all the salad ingredients and mix with the dressing. Spoon the rice salad onto the mushrooms, pressing down firmly. Chill and wrap in cellophane for carrying.

8 open mushrooms
100g Sharwood's Basmati Rice, cooked (4oz)
50g raisins (2oz)
½ green pepper, chopped
1 small can Sharwood's Pimientos, drained, chopped
Dressing:
    Juice from Pimientos
    3 tablespoons lemon juice
    1 tablespoon Sharwood's Mango Chutney
    1 heaped teaspoon Sharwood's Mild or Medium Curry Powder

Serves 8 as an accompaniment.

Preeti Kebabs

Mix meat, onion, garlic, curry paste and parsley together. Divide into 16 and shape into little nuggets. Whisk the egg whites and coat each nugget with the egg white. Fry in the oil until golden and cooked through. Serve with onion rings.

500g minced cooked or raw lamb (1lb)
1 medium onion, chopped
4 cloves garlic, crushed
4 teaspoons Sharwood's Mild or Hot Curry Paste
2 tablespoons Parsley
2 egg whites, beaten
Oil for frying
1 onion sliced

Serves 8 as an accompaniment

Sweet Lassi

Whisk or liquidize together for 2 minutes. Transport in Thermos. Serve in glasses with cardamom sprinkled on froth.

1 large carton natural yoghurt
250ml milk (½ pint)
250ml crushed ice (½ pint)
Few drops rose water
1 tablespoon caster sugar
Ground cardamom

17

GOURMET

Guavas Alaska

Bake blind 6 × 10cm (4 inch) thin pastry circles. Brush with egg white. Place guavas on the pastry bases. Whisk egg whites gradually adding sugar until very stiff. Partially mask guavas, bake 15-20 minutes (200°C, 400°F, Gas Mark 6).

250g rich shortcrust pastry (8oz)
1 egg white, beaten
1 can Sharwood's Guava Halves
3 egg whites
150g caster sugar (6oz)

Serves 6.

Apple Assam

Gently fry onion, apple and Curry Powder, for 5 minutes. Add the potatoes, water and sherry and simmer for 25 minutes. Purée and reheat gently. Serve with a swirl of natural yoghurt and onions.

75g butter (3oz)
1 medium onion, chopped
3 cooking apples, peeled cored and diced
1 heaped teaspoon Sharwood's Hot or Extra Hot Curry Powder
4 potatoes, peeled and diced
125ml water (¼ pint)
2 tablespoons sherry
6 tablespoons natural yoghurt
1 teaspoon salt
Sharwood's dried onions from Onion Bhajia Mix, toasted

Serves 6.

Clementine Duck

Using a sharp knife, slice the meat away from the bone, starting at the central backbone and working down each side. When the knuckle joints are reached, break the bone away. Cut the rib bones with scissors, and pull cage away. Mix stuffing and place in the cavity. Reshape duck securing top and bottom with wooden cocktail sticks. Prick the skin thoroughly. Roast 1½-2 hours (200°C, 400°F, Gas Mark 6). Garnish with the orange and lime slices.

1 large duck 2½-3kg (5-6lb)
Stuffing:
1 onion, diced
2 cloves garlic, crushed
3 tomatoes, chopped
150g Sharwood's Basmati Rice, cooked (6oz)
1 heaped teaspoon Sharwood's Mild or Medium Curry Powder
100g duck or chicken livers, chopped (4oz)
Grated rind and juice of one orange
Grated rind and juice of one lime
1 teaspoon salt
Garnish:
1 orange, sliced
1 lime, sliced

Serves 6 as a main dish.

Cauliflower Pakoras

Split the cauliflower into florets. Mix the Bhajia spices with water. Dip cauliflower in batter and deep fry small batches at a time. (Use the onions from the Onion Bhajias to garnish the soup).

1 packet Sharwood's Onion Bhajia Mix
1 cauliflower
Oil for deep frying

Serves 6 as an accompaniment.

COCKTAILS

Onion Bhajias

Prepare according to the packet instructions.

1 packet Sharwood's Onion Bhajia Mix
Oil for deep frying

Chicken Snacks

Cut the chicken into small pieces. Mix with spice, onion, garlic and salt. Marinate for 4 hours. Mix the gram flour, salt, baking powder and water. Dip batches of chicken into batter, lower into extremely hot oil, reduce heat and continue cooking for 10 minutes.

500g chicken breast, diced (1lb)
2 heaped teaspoons Sharwood's Garam Masala
2 onions, grated
2 cloves garlic, crushed
2 teaspoons salt
Batter:
*   7 tablespoons gram flour*
*   ½ teaspoon salt*
*   ½ teaspoon baking powder*
*   7 tablespoons water*
Oil for deep frying

Serves 10 for cocktails or 6 as main dish with accompaniments.

Tandoori Lamb Kebabs

Thread liver and bacon onto wooden cocktail sticks. Marinate several hours, drain and grill 10-15 minutes basting with butter.

500g lamb's liver diced (1lb)
100g bacon (4oz)
Marinade:
*   1 sachet Sharwood's Tandoori Spice Mix or 3*
*   heaped teaspoons from the orange drum*
*   3 tablespoons each of plain yoghurt, vinegar,*
*   lemon juice and oil*
*   100g butter (4oz)*

Serves 10 for cocktails or 6 as a main dish with accompaniments.

Prawn Cutlets

Peel and devein the prawns, leaving tails on. Slit down the back almost in half. Press open. Coat in paste and oil, leave for 2 hours. Shake off the excess marinade. Coat in egg and breadcrumbs. Fry until golden. Sprinkle with lemon rind just before serving.

10-12 large Pacific prawns
4 heaped teaspoons Sharwood's Vindaloo Curry Paste
2 tablespoons oil
250g fine breadcrumbs (8oz)
2 eggs, beaten
Oil for deep frying
Rind of 1 lemon

Serves 10 for cocktails or 6 as a vegetable accompaniment.

Potato Roulade

Skin the potatoes, and beat in electric mixer 5 minutes or 'process' until very sticky and elastic. Add salt, onion and parsley. Roll out to an oblong 15cm × 20cm (6 inches × 8 inches). Spread with filling and roll up. Chill. Cut in 10-12 slices and fry till golden.

Potato Pastry:
*   1 kg potatoes, boiled in skins (2lb)*
*   1 teaspoon salt*
*   1 onion, finely chopped*
*   1 tablespoon parsley, chopped*
Filling:
*   100g frozen spinach, thawed (4oz)*
*   75g cream cheese (3oz)*
*   1 heaped teaspoon Sharwood's Mild or Hot*
*   Curry Paste*
*   1 teaspoon lemon juice*
Oil for frying

Serves 10 for cocktails or 6 as a vegetable accompaniment.

VEGETARIAN

Mini Puris

Make up according to the packet instructions, but half size.

1 packet of Sharwood's Chapati Paratha and Puri Mix
Water
Oil

Serves 6 as an accompaniment.

Masoor Dall

Cover and simmer the lentils, water and salt together for 1½-2 hours. Until nearly all the liquid has gone. Fry onion in ⅓ of the butter, with Curry Spices. Stir into the lentils. Simmer for 10 minutes. Divide into 6 dishes and pour the remaining melted butter on top of each dish. Garnish with coriander.

250g lentils, washed (8oz)
1 litre water (2 pints)
1 teaspoon salt
150g butter (6oz)
1 large onion, sliced
1 heaped teaspoon Sharwood's Hot or Extra Hot Curry Powder
Fresh coriander leaves

Serves 6 as an accompaniment.

Rice with Chick Peas

Cook the rice in salted water 5 minutes. Drain. In a flame-proof casserole, heat the oil, add the spices and heat for 10-20 seconds. Stir in onions, rice and chick peas, fry 2-3 minutes. Place butter in small knobs on top of the rice. Cover with a sheet of foil and then the lid. Bake in the oven for 45 minutes at 180°C, 350°F, Gas Mark 4.

150g Sharwood's Basmati Rice (6oz)
1 teaspoon salt
2 tablespoons oil
1 heaped teaspoon Sharwood's Mild or Medium Curry Powder
4 onions, sliced
1 teaspoon Sharwood's Garam Masala
150g chick peas, canned (6oz)
75g butter (3oz)

Serves 6 as an accompaniment.

Banana Masala

Coat the bananas in the natural yoghurt and sprinkle with the Garam Masala. Serve chilled.

2 bananas, peeled and sliced
6 tablespoons natural yoghurt
1 teaspoon Sharwood's Garam Masala

Serves 6.

Marrow Kofta Curry

Mix marrow, flour, Garam Masala and salt. Form into 6 patties. Place on a plate, cover with absorbent paper and chill for 2 hours. Fry until golden brown both sides. Drain. Heat vegetables and curry and lay patties on top. Cook gently for 15 minutes. Serve with a sprinkling of Garam Masala.

¾kg marrow flesh, grated (1½lb)
4 tablespoons gram flour or plain flour
2 heaped teaspoons Sharwood's Garam Masala
1 teaspoon salt
Oil for shallow frying
1 can Sharwood's Vegetable Curry
Pinch Sharwood's Garam Masala

Serves 6 as an accompaniment.

Vegetable Samosa

Cook the Curry Paste, potatoes, peas, coriander, salt and Garam Masala in the butter for 10 minutes. Cool. Mix the flour, salt and oil. Stir in the water to make a firm dough. Divide into 9 equal balls. Roll each out to 5 inch circles. Cut each in half. Moisten the edges of each semi circle. Shape one at a time into a cone, fill with a little of the filling and seal the top edge. Repeat until all are filled. Fry the samosas in the hot oil until golden. Serve hot or cold.

50g butter (2oz)
2 heaped teaspoons Sharwood's Mild or Hot Curry Paste
500g potatoes, cooked and diced (1lb)
100g peas (4oz)
1 tablespoon coriander leaves, chopped
½ teaspoon salt
1 teaspoon Sharwood's Garam Masala
250g wholemeal flour (8oz)
1 teaspoon salt
3 tablespoons oil
250ml water (8fl oz)
Oil for deep frying

Serves 6 as a snack or as an accompaniment.